THIS BOOK BELONGS TO

Made in the USA
Monee, IL
14 March 2022

92900395R00056